Ankita Rossi

AF355139

Loire Radweg
(Loire Cycle Path)

Title: Loire Radweg (Loire Cycle Path)
Author: Ankita Rossi
Published by: NEXTUNICORN PUBLISHER PROPRIETORSHIP
Publisher's Address: Shree Dwarkadhish Ji Ka Was, Emri, Rajsamand, RAJASTHAN, India. Pincode: 313342
Printer Details: Published online on various platforms.
Edition: 01
ISBN: 978-81-968464-3-5
© 2023 Ankita Rossi. All rights reserved.
Images Source: Pixbay: (https://pixabay.com/)
All images' rights belong to their respective owners.
Disclaimer: The author and publisher disclaim all liability for accuracy, loss, or damage arising from the use of this travel guide; users are urged to independently verify information and prioritize personal safety.

Catalog

Welcome to the Loire Radweg!

Cultural Riches:

As you embark on the enchanting Loire Radweg, a remarkable journey awaits, unveiling a tapestry of cultural marvels. While many may sing praises of bustling cities, the Loire Radweg holds its own treasures, inviting you to discover its rich cultural heritage.

Quaint Villages: The Hidden Jewels:

Along your path on the Loire Radweg, you will stumble upon charming villages that seem straight out of a fairytale. Each village carries its own unique story, with medieval castles, picturesque chapels, and cobblestone streets that echo centuries of history. These hidden gems offer a glimpse into different chapters of the past at every turn.

Châteaux Along the Loire: Architectural Grandeur:

The Loire Radweg showcases architectural wonders of its own. The châteaux that line this route stand as testaments to France's illustrious history and architectural prowess. From the enchanting

Château de Chambord resembling something out of a fairytale to the elegant Château de Chenonceau gracefully spanning across the River Cher – each edifice tells a story of royalty, artistry, and cultural opulence.

Blois: A Tapestry of History:

Nestled along the Loire is Blois – a city that breathes life into history itself. The Royal Château de Blois stands as an awe-inspiring blend of Gothic, Renaissance, and Classical architecture – an embodiment of political intrigue and artistic brilliance throughout time. Take leisurely strolls along cobbled streets and let yourself be enchanted by Maison de la Magie as it adds an air of magic to your cultural journey.

Saumur: Equestrian Elegance:

Another gem along the Loire Radweg is Saumur with its renowned equestrian traditions. The Cadre Noir, the National Equestrian School, stands as a testament to this legacy. Immerse yourself in the world of horsemanship and witness the grace and elegance of these majestic creatures against the backdrop of Saumur's historic charm.

Gastronomic Pleasures:

The Loire Radweg not only reveals architectural wonders but also takes you on a culinary odyssey through the heart of France. From the vineyards of Sancerre to the mouthwatering goat cheeses of Chavignol, every bite tells a story of terroir and tradition.

Wine and Terroir: A Perfect Pairing:

Indulge your senses in the world of Loire Valley wines. The vineyards that adorn this route produce an exquisite array of wines – from the crisp Sauvignon Blancs of Sancerre to the elegant Cabernet Francs of Chinon. Take a detour to explore cellars, meet passionate winemakers, and savor every sip that encapsulates the essence of this unique terroir.

Immerse yourself in vibrant local markets along the Loire Radweg. From bustling markets in Tours to quaint stalls in Amboise, these culinary havens offer a kaleidoscope of flavors. Sample artisanal cheeses, freshly baked breads, and succulent fruits – each market is a celebration showcasing local produce and gastronomic delights.

Scenic Landscapes:

As you pedal along on your journey along the Loire Radweg, breathtaking landscapes unfold before your eyes. The riverbanks adorned with wildflowers create a mesmerizing backdrop for your adventure. From rolling vineyards to serene meanders along the Loire River itself – this route is truly nature's symphony at its finest.

Welcome to a world where history, culture, gastronomy, and natural beauty intertwine along the enchanting Loire Radweg. Embark on this unforgettable journey and let it ignite your senses as you immerse yourself in its captivating allure.

1. Château de Chambord:

Château de Chambord, a masterpiece of the French Renaissance, was originally constructed in the 16th century as a hunting lodge for King Francis I. It showcases an exquisite blend of medieval and classical architecture.

There are several key attractions that make Château de Chambord worth visiting. You can marvel at the double helix staircase, which is truly a sight to behold. The rooftop terraces offer panoramic views that will leave you in awe. And let's not forget about the vast hunting grounds surrounding the château.

If you're wondering when is the best time to visit, I would recommend spring or fall. During these seasons, you can enjoy mild weather and avoid large crowds.

The opening hours of Château de Chambord vary depending on the season. Generally, it is open from 9:00 AM to 6:00 PM.

For more information or inquiries, you can contact them at +33 2 54 50 40 00.

To explore some hidden gems within the château's vicinity, consider taking a bike ride through its extensive grounds or embarking on a boat ride along the canal for a unique perspective. When it comes to culinary delights, don't miss out on indulging in local delicacies at the on-site restaurant. They offer a taste of Loire Valley cuisine that will surely satisfy your palate.

If you want to learn more about Château de Chambord and plan your visit accordingly, check out their official website [here](https://www.chambord.org/en).

---

2. Château de Chenonceau:

Château de Chenonceau, also known as the "Ladies' Castle," holds a rich history dating back to the 16th century when it was built over the River Cher. Throughout its existence, this magnificent castle has been shaped by influential women.

When you visit, be prepared to be amazed by the stunning architecture, take leisurely strolls through the beautiful gardens, and explore the historic chambers that hold tales of the past.

To make the most of your visit, consider going in spring when the gardens are in full bloom or during fall when there are fewer crowds.

The opening hours of Château de Chenonceau vary depending on the season but generally start at 9:30 AM and end at 5:30 PM. For more detailed information, you can reach them at +33 2 47 23 90 07.

If you want to dive deeper into the castle's charm, don't miss out on visiting the Flower Workshop. Here you can witness floral artistry inspired by the gardens of Château de Chenonceau.

To satisfy your taste buds with delightful French cuisine while enjoying a riverside view, make sure to dine at L'Orangerie. This hidden gem offers a culinary experience that perfectly complements your visit to Château de Chenonceau.

For additional details and planning your trip to this enchanting castle, feel free to visit their official website [Château de Chenonceau](https://www.chenonceau.com/en/).

---

3. Château de Villandry:

Château de Villandry, a magnificent structure that was constructed in the 16th century, is widely recognized for its meticulously designed Renaissance gardens. These gardens showcase an intricate geometric precision that is truly remarkable. When you visit Château de Villandry, there are several key attractions that you must explore. One of the highlights is the ornamental gardens themselves, which are a sight to behold. In addition to that, you can also venture inside the château to admire its stunning interiors. And let's not forget about the charming village of Villandry, which adds a touch of quaint beauty to the whole experience.

To fully appreciate the beauty of the gardens at Château de Villandry, it is recommended to visit during late spring when everything is in full bloom. This will provide you with a truly enchanting and colorful spectacle.

The opening hours of Château de Villandry vary depending on the season. Generally, it opens at 9:00 AM and closes at 6:30 PM. It's always a good idea to check their official website or contact them directly for more accurate information. You can reach them at +33 2 47 50 02 09.

If you're looking for something extra special and magical, I highly recommend attending the Evening Candlelit Visits at Château de Villandry. This unique experience will transport you to another world as you explore the enchanting grounds illuminated by candlelight.

And when it comes to satisfying your taste buds, look no further than the on-site restaurant at Château de Villandry. Not only does it offer delicious regional dishes, but it also provides a breathtaking view of the gardens while you dine.

In conclusion, visiting Château de Villandry promises an unforgettable journey through time and nature's beauty. Make sure to plan your trip accordingly and take advantage of all the hidden gems that this place has to offer.

Blois has a captivating history, with the Royal Château de Blois serving as a regal residence for numerous French kings. The key attractions include exploring the royal chambers, enjoying the mesmerizing sound and light show, and strolling through the charming old town of Blois. If you plan to visit, summer is the perfect time to witness the enchanting Blois "Nuits Solaires" light show. The opening hours of the Château vary by season, but it generally opens from 9:00 AM to 6:30 PM. For further information or inquiries, you can contact them at +33 2 54 90 33 33. To learn more about this historical gem, you can visit their official website [Château de Blois](http://en.chateaudeblois.fr/). Apart from these well-known attractions, there are also hidden gems to explore in Blois like Maison de la Magie, a fascinating museum dedicated to magic and illusion. And if you're a food enthusiast, don't miss out on indulging in local specialties at the quaint cafes that line the streets of the old town.

Saumur, with its castle deeply intertwined in a rich history, has witnessed significant events during the Hundred Years' War. If you're planning a visit, make sure to explore Saumur Castle, immerse yourself in the elegance of the Cadre Noir, and wander through the charming Old Town. To enjoy pleasant weather, it's recommended to plan your trip during spring or early fall. The opening hours of various attractions vary but generally range from 10:00 AM to 6:00 PM. For more information or inquiries, you can contact +33 2 41 40 24 40 or visit the official website of Saumur Tourist Office at https://www.ot-saumur.fr/en/. In addition to the well-known attractions, don't miss out on exploring the hidden gems of Saumur Castle - delve into its underground tunnels and get a captivating glimpse into its military history. And when it comes to culinary delights, make sure to savor the local wines at Saumur's vineyards and indulge in traditional dishes at local bistros.

Amboise, a town steeped in history and known for its Royal Château, holds great significance as a favored royal residence. It has a charm that draws visitors from all over. When you explore Amboise, make sure to visit the majestic château, immerse yourself in the beauty of Clos Lucé, and take in the breathtaking panoramic views from the Château's terraces.

To truly experience the essence of Amboise, plan your visit during spring when the gardens are in full bloom or summer when outdoor events add to the vibrant atmosphere. The opening hours of these attractions may vary by season but generally start at 9:00 AM and end at 7:00 PM.

For any inquiries or further information, you can reach out to them at +33 2 47 57 00 73. To stay updated with all things related to Château d'Amboise, you can visit their official website at [Château d'Amboise](https://www.chateau-amboise.com/en/).

Apart from the well-known attractions, there are hidden gems waiting to be discovered in Amboise. One such gem is Clos Lucé, which was Leonardo da Vinci's final residence. Explore this fascinating place and delve into da Vinci's world.

When it comes to culinary delights, Amboise doesn't disappoint. Indulge in local cuisine offered by restaurants along the picturesque Loire River. Not only will you savor delicious food but also enjoy a scenic dining experience that perfectly complements your visit to this charming town.

7. Azay-le-Rideau:

Château d'Azay-le-Rideau, a castle that was constructed in the 16th century, is a remarkable example of French Renaissance architecture. It possesses an enchanting appearance, surrounded by water, resembling something out of a fairytale.

One of the main attractions of this castle is the breathtaking reflection it casts on the Indre River. Visitors can also explore the interior, which is adorned with period furnishings that provide a glimpse into history. Additionally, taking a leisurely stroll through the beautiful gardens surrounding the castle is highly recommended.

To fully enjoy your visit to Château d'Azay-le-Rideau, it is advisable to plan your trip during late spring or early fall when you can experience pleasant weather and witness the gardens in full bloom.

The opening hours of Château d'Azay-le-Rideau vary by season and are generally from 9:30 AM to 6:30 PM. For more information or inquiries, you can contact them at +33 2 47 45 42 04. You may also visit their official website [here](https://www.azay-le-rideau.fr/en).

Apart from its well-known highlights, there are hidden gems that make visiting this castle even more special. One such gem is attending the evening sound and light show, where you can immerse yourself in a magical experience that will leave you spellbound.

When it comes to culinary delights, exploring local eateries in the nearby town should not be missed. These establishments offer traditional French cuisine that will tantalize your taste buds and complete your visit with an authentic gastronomic experience.

---

8. Villandry:

Welcome to the charming village of Villandry, renowned for its historical and agricultural significance. One of its main highlights is the magnificent Château de Villandry and its stunning Renaissance gardens. These meticulously designed ornamental gardens are a sight to behold, especially during late spring when they are in full bloom.

Apart from exploring the castle and its gardens, take some time to immerse yourself in the village's rich history and architectural charm. You can also enjoy a panoramic view from the castle, which offers breathtaking vistas of the surrounding area.

If you plan on visiting, keep in mind that the opening hours may vary depending on the season. Generally, you can explore from 9:00 AM to 6:30 PM. For any inquiries or additional information, you can contact them at +33 2 47 50 02 09 or visit their official website [Château de Villandry](http://www.chateauvillandry.fr/en/).

For a truly magical experience, don't miss out on attending one of their Evening Candlelit Visits. This enchanting event adds an extra layer of charm to your visit.

After strolling through the gardens and immersing yourself in history, treat yourself to some culinary delights at the château's restaurant. From there, you can savor local cuisine while enjoying a picturesque view overlooking the beautiful gardens.

---

9. Fontevraud Abbey:

Fontevraud Abbey, a site recognized by UNESCO as a World Heritage, holds a rich history that can be traced back to the 12th century. It served as the final resting place for esteemed royalty, including Richard the Lionheart.

When you explore this remarkable abbey, you'll be captivated by its stunning Gothic architecture and the presence of Plantagenet tombs. The serene atmosphere adds to the overall charm of this place.

You can plan your visit throughout the year, but if you want to witness blooming gardens, spring would be an ideal time.

The opening hours of Fontevraud Abbey are from 9:00 AM to 6:30 PM, although these may vary depending on the season. If you need more information or have any inquiries, feel free to contact them at +33 2 41 51 73 52.

For further details and official updates about Fontevraud Abbey, you can visit their website: [Fontevraud Abbey](https://www.fontevraud.fr/en).

Apart from its well-known attractions, there are hidden gems waiting to be discovered at this abbey. Cultural events and concerts are hosted here regularly, offering visitors unique experiences.

To satisfy your taste buds during your visit, don't miss out on dining at the on-site restaurant. They offer a delightful blend of traditional and contemporary cuisine that will surely leave you satisfied with culinary delights.

Château de Cheverny, renowned for its exquisitely preserved interiors, boasts a rich history that dates back to the 17th century and remains under the ownership of the esteemed Hurault family. This majestic establishment offers a myriad of captivating attractions, including the opportunity to immerse yourself in the opulence of its interiors, indulge in the Tintin exhibition, and wander through the meticulously maintained grounds that envelop the château. To make the most of your visit, it is advisable to plan your trip during spring or fall when you can relish pleasant weather and avoid large crowds. The opening hours vary depending on the season but generally start from 9:15 AM until 6:30 PM. For further information or inquiries, you can contact Château de Cheverny at +33 2 54 79 96 29. Additionally, you may explore their official website [here](https://www.chateau-cheverny.fr/en/) for more details. As you delve deeper into this enchanting destination, don't miss out on some hidden gems such as visiting the kennels to witness firsthand how hunting hounds are fed. And when it comes to satisfying your taste buds with culinary delights, venture into the neighboring village where an array of local eateries await, ready to tantalize your palate with their regional specialties.

---

11. Montlouis-sur-Loire:

Montlouis-sur-Loire, nestled along the scenic Loire River, has a rich history dating back to Roman times. It is renowned for its vineyards and wine production.

When you visit this charming destination, you can immerse yourself in picturesque landscapes, indulge in delightful wine tasting sessions at local vineyards, and experience the tranquility of the riverside.

The best time to plan your visit is during late spring or early fall when the weather is pleasant, and the vineyards are in full bloom. Keep in mind that the opening hours may vary for each individual vineyard, so it's advisable to check with them directly for specific details.

One of the hidden gems of Montlouis-sur-Loire is its vibrant wine festivals. Attending these festivals will give you a chance to celebrate and appreciate the region's viticulture in all its glory.

To enhance your culinary experience, make sure to pair local wines with artisanal cheeses and other delectable treats available in this charming destination.

regional delicacies at vineyard tastings.

Let's delve into the captivating history of the medieval Château de Langeais, a remarkable fortress boasting an impressive drawbridge that has stood the test of time since the 15th century. This magnificent structure played a significant role in the legendary Hundred Years' War.

As you explore this architectural gem, prepare to be enchanted by its well-preserved interiors and immerse yourself in the charming medieval ambiance that permeates every corner. The drawbridge itself is a sight to behold, offering a glimpse into ancient times.

To make the most of your visit, plan to come during late spring or early fall when the weather is mild and crowds are fewer. Keep in mind that opening hours may vary depending on the season, but generally, you can enjoy this historical treasure from 9:30 AM to 6:00 PM.

If you need any further information or have any inquiries, feel free to contact +33 2 47 96 72 60. For additional details and updates, be sure to visit the official website of Château de Langeais at http://www.chateau-de-langeais.com/en/.

Beyond its well-known attractions, Château de Langeais holds hidden gems that transport visitors back in time through captivating historical reenactments. Immerse yourself in vivid depictions of days gone by and gain a deeper understanding of this remarkable era.

Indulge your taste buds with culinary delights as you explore local cafes and bakeries nestled within Langeais. These establishments offer an array of traditional French pastries and cuisine that will leave you craving for more.

So why wait? Embark on an unforgettable journey through history at Château de Langeais and create memories that will last a lifetime!

Currency:
The currency used along the Loire Radweg is the Euro (€).
Language:
French is the official language along the Loire Radweg.
Time:
The Loire Radweg operates in Central European Time (CET), which is GMT/UTC plus one hour. It's important to be aware of the time difference when scheduling activities and making travel arrangements.
Emergency Numbers:
In case of emergencies along the Loire Radweg, here are some important contact numbers:
- Ambulance: 112
- Police: 17
- Fire: 18
When calling from outside the region, remember to dial your international access code followed by France's country code (%33) and then the number (including the '0').
Useful Websites:
While traveling along the Loire Radweg, you can make use of these online resources:
- SNCF (www.sncf.com): The official website for French national railways, providing train travel information.
- Gîtes de France (www.gites-de-france.com): Explore rural accommodations for a unique lodging experience.
- Slow Food (www.slowfood.com): Discover local producers, restaurants, and markets, immersing yourself in culinary delights.
- France.fr (www.france.fr): The official website of France Tourism, offering comprehensive travel information.
Daily Costs:
Here's a breakdown of daily costs along the Loire Radweg:
- Budget (Less than €100): Traveling on a budget? Hostel dorm beds range from €15-30, while budget hotel double rooms range

from €50 to €110. Affordable meals at local establishments typically cost between €6 and €12.

- Midrange (€100–€250): If you're looking for midrange options, double rooms in hotels cost between €110 and €200. Meals at local restaurants average around €25 to €50 per meal, and attraction admissions range from €4 to €15.

- Top End (More than €250): Luxury travelers can find options with double rooms in four- or five-star hotels ranging from €200 to €450. Dining at high-end restaurants may cost between €50 and €150 per person, offering exceptional culinary experiences.

Opening Hours:

Opening hours along the Loire Radweg can vary by season. Here are some general guidelines:

- Banks: 9am–1pm and 3pm–5pm, Monday to Friday
- Restaurants: Noon–2:30pm and 7:30pm–11pm or midnight
- Cafes: 8am–8pm
- Shops: 9am–1pm and 4pm–8pm, Monday to Saturday

Arriving along the Loire Radweg:

Depending on your arrival point along the Loire Radweg, you'll likely arrive at major transportation hubs. Here are some key options:

- Nantes Atlantique Airport: Consider shuttle services or taxis for transportation to the city center.

- Tours Val de Loire Airport: Options include shuttle buses, taxis, or rental cars for transport to the Loire Valley.

- Angers Loire Airport: Taxis or rental cars are convenient choices for reaching your destination in the Loire Valley.

- Paris Charles de Gaulle Airport: High-speed trains from the airport provide swift access to major cities along the Loire Radweg. With all these practical details, you're well-equipped to explore the beautiful landscapes, cultural heritage, and delightful experiences along the Loire Radweg. Enjoy your journey!

Loire Valley Discovery - 2 Weeks

Embarking on your journey through the Loire Radweg in the vibrant city of Nantes is a great way to start. Take your time exploring the historic Château des Ducs de Bretagne and wandering through the picturesque streets of the Bouffay district. Immerse yourself in the contemporary art scene at Les Machines de l'île.

As you proceed to Angers, known for its medieval castle and vibrant cultural scene, you'll enter a new phase of your adventure. Explore the historic Tapestry of the Apocalypse and indulge in local cuisine at the lively Marché des Capucins. Taking a scenic stroll along the Maine River will allow you to truly appreciate the charm of this city.

Venturing into Saumur, famed for its impressive château and association with cavalry, will add another layer of excitement to your trip. Don't miss out on visiting the renowned Cadre Noir equestrian school and enjoying a leisurely boat ride on the Loire River. Exploring troglodyte caves and savoring local wines from surrounding vineyards are experiences that shouldn't be missed.

Tours offers an artistic charm like no other, with splendid Renaissance architecture adorning its streets. A visit to Musée des Beaux-Arts is highly recommended, as is strolling through historic Place Plumereau. Delight in regional gastronomy at local bistros and make sure to explore Château de Villandry's iconic ornamental gardens nearby.

Concluding your Loire Radweg adventure in Orleans will be a memorable experience. This city steeped in history invites you to discover Joan of Arc's legacy at Place du Martroi while wandering through medieval streets filled with stories waiting to be told. Indulge in local delicacies at vibrant Les Halles market and savor the last moments of your journey along the beautiful Loire.

Commence your exploration in the picturesque town of Amboise, where the Royal Château d'Amboise dominates the landscape. Make sure to visit Clos Lucé, which was Leonardo da Vinci's final residence, and enjoy a scenic walk along the Loire River. Immerse yourself in the artistic and historical richness that this region has to offer.

Heading to Blois, where the Royal Château de Blois awaits with its stunning blend of architectural styles, will be a treat for your senses. Explore the historic streets and vibrant markets while delving into the city's cultural heritage at Maison de la Magie. Don't forget to take in panoramic views from the castle's terraces.

Marveling at the grandeur of Château de Chambord, which is known as the largest château in the Loire Valley, is an experience like no other. Delve into intricate details of French Renaissance architecture and explore the expansive park surrounding this majestic structure. Enjoy leisurely bike rides through serene countryside landscapes.

As you proceed to "Ladies' Castle," Château de Chenonceau spanning over River Cher, prepare to be enchanted by its beauty. Explore enchanting gardens and immerse yourself in history as you discover more about this iconic château. Taking a tranquil boat ride on the river will allow you to fully appreciate its idyllic surroundings.

Concluding your journey in Villandry will leave you with memories of exquisite Renaissance gardens that are renowned worldwide. Wander through meticulously designed ornamental gardens and explore charming villages nearby. Appreciate how art, nature, and history harmoniously blend together in defining what makes Loire Valley truly special.

When it comes to accommodation options along the Loire Radweg, there is a wide variety to choose from, each offering a unique and immersive experience. Whether you're drawn to the charm of countryside retreats or prefer the convenience of modern hotels, the Loire Valley caters to all tastes and budgets. Here are some essential tips and a comprehensive guide to help you find the perfect place to stay along the Loire Radweg:

1. Booking in Advance:

  - While the Loire Radweg is not as crowded as some popular Italian destinations, it's still advisable to book your accommodations in advance, especially during peak seasons like spring and summer. Charming bed and breakfasts and boutique hotels can fill up quickly.

2. Seasonal Price Fluctuations:

  - Accommodation rates in the Loire Valley may vary depending on the season. Summer, when the region is in full bloom, tends to be a peak tourist time. Spring and early fall offer pleasant weather and potentially more budget-friendly rates.

3. Price Depends on Location:

  - The Loire Valley encompasses a diverse range of landscapes, from riverside towns to vineyard-dotted countryside. Accommodation costs can vary based on location. Consider your preferences – whether it's staying in a quaint village or opting for a city hotel – and plan accordingly.

4. Charming B&Bs:

  - Bed and Breakfasts in the Loire Valley are often charming establishments, ranging from historic farmhouses to urban residences. Prices can vary, with budget-friendly options starting around €40-€80 per night, while more luxurious choices may range from €100-€150 or more.

5. Campgrounds amid Nature:

  - Campgrounds in the Loire Valley offer a unique opportunity to connect with nature. Prices for campsites typically range from

€15-€30 per night. Some campgrounds may offer all-inclusive options, while others charge separately for amenities.

6. Unique Convents and Monasteries:

  - For a distinctive experience, consider staying in a convent or monastery along the Loire Radweg. While some prioritize spiritual retreats, others rent rooms to travelers. Prices are generally reasonable, providing a serene and culturally rich environment.

7. Charming Hostels for Budget Travel:

  - Hostels in the Loire Valley provide budget-friendly options, especially for solo travelers or those seeking a social atmosphere. Prices for hostel beds range from €20-€40 per night, with additional options for private rooms.

8. Hotel & Pensioni Options:

  - Hotels in the Loire Valley vary from quaint pensioni to upscale establishments. Prices for single rooms can start from €50, while double rooms may range from €80-€150, depending on the location and amenities. Pensioni are often slightly more budget-friendly.

9. Mountain Huts in Scenic Settings:

  - If you're exploring the mountainous regions along the Loire Radweg, consider staying in mountain huts. Prices for mountain huts, especially those operated by local alpine clubs, can range from €25-€40 per person.

10. Rental Accommodations for Flexibility:

  - Rental options include apartments and studios. For short stays, prices can vary with an average cost of €70-€120 per night. Monthly rentals may offer more competitive rates starting from €800-€1200.

11. Villas for a Luxurious Experience:

  - Villas in the Loire Valley provide an indulgent experience often surrounded by vineyards or near historic towns. Prices for villa rentals can range from €150-€500 or more per night offering a luxurious retreat.

Visas and Residency along the Loire Radweg

Embarking on a journey along the Loire Radweg requires a good understanding of the visa and residency regulations. Let me provide you with a comprehensive guide that will help you navigate through the entry and stay requirements for your trip through the beautiful Loire Valley.

1. Schengen Treaty for European Citizens:

   - If you are a European citizen from one of the countries that are part of the Schengen Treaty, you can freely travel along the Loire Radweg as long as you have a valid identity card or passport.

2. Visa Exemptions for Select Countries:

   - Travelers from various non-EU countries, including but not limited to Australia, Brazil, Canada, Israel, Japan, New Zealand, and the USA, can explore the stunning Loire Valley without needing a visa for up to 90 days for tourism purposes. However, it's important to check specific requirements and exemptions, especially if you plan on visiting the UK or Ireland.

3. Visas for Non-EU and Non-Schengen Nationals:

   - If you are a non-EU or non-Schengen national planning to stay in the Loire Valley for more than 90 days or for purposes other than tourism (such as work or study), you may need specific visas.

   - For detailed information on visa requirements that may vary based on individual circumstances, it is best to visit the official website www.esteri.it/visti/home_eng.asp or contact an Italian consulate.

4. Residence and Work for EU Citizens:

   - EU citizens can reside and work in the captivating Loire Valley without needing permits initially. However, after three months of their stay, they must register at their local municipal registry office by providing proof of work or sufficient financial means.

5. Permanent Residence for Non-EU Foreign Citizens:

   - Non-EU foreign citizens who have continuously resided in the Loire Valley for five years can apply for permanent residence status.

6. Permesso di Soggiorno (Permit to Stay):
 - If you are a non-EU citizen planning to stay in one location along the Loire Radweg for more than one week, it is important to obtain a 'permesso di soggiorno' from the local police station.
 - However, if you are staying in hotels as a tourist, you are generally exempt from this requirement.
 - The 'permesso di soggiorno' becomes necessary if you plan to study, work, or have an extended residence. You can obtain it from the police, but please note that the application process may be complex and requires specific documents. For the latest requirements under 'Foreign nationals,' check www.poliziadistato.it.
 - EU citizens do not need to obtain a 'permesso di soggiorno.'
7. Study Visas:
 - Non-EU citizens planning to study along the Loire Radweg at a local university or language school must apply for a study visa at the nearest Italian embassy or consulate.
 - Requirements typically include proof of enrollment, fee payment, and sufficient funds to support yourself during your study period.
 - Study visas are issued for the duration of enrollment and can be renewed within the Loire Valley upon providing proof of ongoing studies and financial means.
Understanding these visa and residency intricacies is crucial for ensuring a seamless and lawful journey along the enchanting Loire Radweg. Stay informed by consulting official sources so that your travel plans align with the latest regulations.

Section 1: Starting Point - Nevers to Decize
- Distance: Approximately 40 km
- Key Landmarks:
  - Begin your journey in the historic city of Nevers, famous for its cathedral and vibrant markets.
  - Cycle through the picturesque village of Apremont-sur-Allier, adorned with stunning floral displays.
  - Conclude this section in Decize, a town with a rich industrial past.
Section 2: Decize to Digoin
- Distance: Around 30 km
- Key Highlights:
  - Follow the scenic Canal lateral à la Loire and enjoy peaceful waterside views.
  - Admire the elegance of Château de la Clayette, surrounded by lush greenery.
  - Explore Digoin and its iconic canal bridge, a testament to engineering brilliance.
Section 3: Digoin to Roanne
- Distance: Approximately 60 km
- Scenic Spots:
  - Pedal along the picturesque Canal de Roanne à Digoin, embraced by nature.
  - Discover the charm of Marcigny with its medieval streets and bustling market.
  - Conclude this section in Roanne, a town that offers a blend of history and contemporary culture.
Section 4: Roanne to Orleans
- Distance: Around 130 km
- Landmarks and Towns:
  - Visit the stunning Château de Sully-sur-Loire in Sully-sur-Loire, one of the highlights along the route.
  - Immerse yourself in the medieval charm of Beaugency with its historic bridge.

- Reach Orleans, a vibrant city rich in Joan of Arc history and lively streets.

Section 5: Orleans to Tours

- Distance: Approximately 120 km
- Noteworthy Stops:
  - Marvel at the grandeur of Château de Chambord, a masterpiece of Renaissance architecture.
  - Cycle through Blois, home to a royal château and enchanting old town streets.
  - Conclude this section in Tours, a city that offers a blend of history, art, and gastronomy.

Section 6: Tours to Saumur

- Distance: Around 70 km
- Scenic Delights:
  - Visit Château de Villandry with its renowned Renaissance gardens in Villandry.
  - Admire the fairytale-like Château d'Azay-le-Rideau surrounded by water in Azay-le-Rideau.
  - Reach Saumur, known for its impressive castle and association with cavalry.

Section 7: Saumur to Angers

- Distance: Approximately 60 km
- Landmarks and Attractions:
  - Explore the serene Fontevraud Abbey, a UNESCO World Heritage site.
  - Cycle through the charming village of Montsoreau along the Loire River.
  - Conclude this section in Angers, home to the impressive Angers Castle.

Section 8: Angers to Nantes

- Distance: Around 90 km
- Final Highlights:
  - Cycle past Oudon and its iconic medieval castle.
  - Explore Champtoceaux, a historic village overlooking the Loire River.
  Reach Nantes, a vibrant city known for its cultural richness and artistic flair.

Elevation Profiles and Difficulty Ratings:
- Each section varies in elevation and difficulty. The route is generally cyclist-friendly with flat stretches along the Loire River. Some sections may include gentle slopes or detours to elevated châteaux.
- Difficulty ratings range from easy to moderate, catering to cyclists of different skill levels. Sections with historical sites may involve short climbs.

Embarking on the Loire Radweg is an exhilarating expedition that takes you through a tapestry of historical landmarks, picturesque towns, and breathtaking landscapes. Here, we present the essential junctions along the route to assist cyclists in navigating this unforgettable journey:

Junction 1: Nevers

- Starting Point: Nevers, a city steeped in history renowned for its majestic cathedral and vibrant markets.

- Directions:

  - Begin your adventure at the central square in Nevers.

  - Follow the signs guiding you towards the scenic path along the meandering Loire River, marking the start of your cycling odyssey.

Junction 2: Decize

- Next Stop: Decize, a town with a fascinating industrial heritage.

- Cycling Route:

  - Continue your journey along the Canal lateral à la Loire while keeping an eye out for signs leading to Decize.

  - Take some time to explore the town's captivating historic center before continuing on your quest.

Junction 3: Digoin

- En Route to: Digoin, a town renowned for its iconic canal bridge.

- Guidance:

  - Pedal alongside the picturesque Canal lateral à la Loire as it meanders through idyllic landscapes.

  - Arrive in Digoin and savor a moment to admire its emblematic canal bridge that stands as a testament to engineering marvel.

Junction 4: Roanne

- Destination: Roanne, where history seamlessly blends with contemporary culture.

- Route Highlights:

  - Cycle along the scenic Canal de Roanne à Digoin, indulging in enchanting waterside vistas throughout your ride.

  - Immerse yourself in medieval charm as you explore Marcigny's winding streets before reaching vibrant Roanne.

Junction 5: Orleans

- Towards Orleans: Sully-sur-Loire, a town renowned for its magnificent Château de Sully-sur-Loire.
- Cycling Path:
  - Follow the signposts guiding you to Sully-sur-Loire, passing through the medieval charm of Beaugency.
  - Continue your journey towards Orleans, a city steeped in rich history and home to the heritage of Joan of Arc.

Junction 6: Tours

- Heading to Tours: Chambord, home to the majestic Château de Chambord.
- Navigational Tips:
  - Pedal through Blois, where a royal château awaits you on your way to Chambord.
  - Arrive in Tours, a city that offers an enticing blend of history and gastronomy for you to savor and explore.

Junction 7: Saumur

- Saumur Bound: Villandry, famous for its Renaissance gardens at the enchanting Château de Villandry.
- Routing Instructions:
  - Make a stop at Azay-le-Rideau and marvel at its fairytale-like château as you continue your journey towards Saumur.
  - Discover Saumur's impressive castle and immerse yourself in its rich equestrian heritage.

Junction 8: Angers

- Towards Angers: Fontevraud Abbey, a tranquil UNESCO World Heritage site.
- Pathway Directions:
  - Cycle through Montsoreau, a charming village nestled along the banks of the Loire River.
  - Conclude this leg of your adventure in Angers, where you'll encounter the awe-inspiring Angers Castle.

Junction 9: Nantes

- Final Destination: Nantes, a vibrant city brimming with cultural richness.
- Final Cycling Stretches:

- Pass by Oudon and its medieval castle, then continue your journey through the captivating village of Champtoceaux.

- Reach Nantes, where your Loire Radweg adventure culminates in an explosion of artistic brilliance.

These key junctions serve as beacons and waypoints, ensuring that cyclists relish a seamless and delightful experience along the Loire Radweg. Enjoy the thrill of cycling!

If you're looking for comfortable lodging options along the Loire Radweg, you've come to the right place. We have two fantastic hotels at each junction, complete with addresses, telephone numbers, and websites for your convenience. Let's dive in!

Junction 1: Nevers

1. Hôtel de Verdun
   - Address: 25 Rue du Pont Cizeau, 58000 Nevers, France
   - Telephone: +33 3 86 36 30 61
   - Website: Check out Hotel de Verdun Nevers
[here](https://www.hoteldeverdun-nevers.com/).

2. Best Western Hotel De Diane
   - Address: 38 Rue du Midi, 58000 Nevers, France
   - Telephone: +33 3 86 68 09 09
   - Website: Explore Best Western De Diane
[here](https://www.bestwestern.fr/en/hotel-Nevers-Best-Western-Hotel-De-Diane-93863).

Junction 2: Decize

1. Le Grand Monarque
   - Address:7 Faubourg de Lorette,58300 Decize ,France
   - Telephone:+33 (0)3.86.77.08.09
    Website:[Le Grand Monarque
Decize](https://www.legrandmonarque.fr/)

2.Hotel de la Poste

Address :4 Avenue de Verdun ,58300 Decize ,France

Telephone :+33 (0)3 .86 .77 .00 .30

Website:[Hotel de la Poste
Decize](https://www.hoteldelapostedecize.com/)

Junction3 : Digoin

1.Le Relais

Address :26 Rue Nationale ,71160 Digoin ,France

Telephone :+ 33 (0) 3.85 .53 .22.72

Website:[Le Relais Digoin](https://www.lerelais-digoin.com/)

2.Hôtel l'Abriche

Address :19 Rue du Pont Canal ,71160 Digoin ,France

Telephone: +33 (0)3 .85 .53. 76.60
Website:[Hotel l'Abriche Digoin](https://hotel-labriche.fr/)
Junction4 : Roanne
1.Ibis Styles Roanne Centre Gare
Address:46 Cours de la République,42300 Roanne,France
Telephone:+33 (0)4.77.23.62.60
Website: Discover Ibis Styles Roanne Centre Gare
[here](https://all.accor.com/hotel/9588/index.fr.shtml)
2.Château de Matel
Address :98 Rue de Matel ,42300 Roanne ,France
Telephone :+33 (0)4 .77 .71 .88 .71
Website:[Château de Matel
Roanne](https://www.chateaudematel.com/)
Junction 5: Tarare
1. The Hôtel Restaurant de la Tour is located at Place de la Gare,
69170 Tarare, France. You can contact them at +33 4 74 63 09 74.
For more information, you can visit their website at [Hotel
Restaurant de la Tour Tarare](https://www.hoteldelatour-
tarare.com/).
2. Another option is the Hotel-Restaurant Saint Romain Logis
situated at 18 Rue de la République, 69170 Tarare, France. Their
telephone number is +33 4 74 63 02 53. To learn more about this
hotel, you can visit their website [Hotel Saint Romain
Tarare](https://www.hotelsaintromain.com/).
Junction 6: Lyon
1. If you're heading towards Lyon, consider staying at the
Radisson Blu Hotel located on 129 Rue Servient, Lyon, France
(69003). You can reach them at +33 4 78 63 55 and find more
information on their website [Radisson Blu
Lyon](https://www.radissonhotels.com/en-us/hotels/radisson-
blu-lyon).
2. Alternatively, there's the Hotel Carlton Lyon - MGallery Hotel
Collection situated at the address of Rue Jussieu, Lyon (69002).
You can contact them at +33-4-78-37-57-31 or check out their
website [Hotel Carlton
Lyon](https://all.accor.com/hotel/0833/index.fr.shtml).
Junction7: Belleville-sur-Saône

1. The Hotel Ibis Villefranche sur Saône offers a comfortable stay and is located on Rue des Prés Pothiers in Villefranche-sur-Saône (69400). Contact them at +33 4 74 68 07 07 or visit their website [Ibis Villefranche sur Saône](https://all.accor.com/hotel/0713/index.fr.shtml).
2. Another option in Belleville-sur-Saône is the Kyriad Villefranche-sur-Saône, situated on Rue de la Sous-Préfecture (69400). You can reach them at +33 4 74 62 17 17 or find more information on their website [Kyriad Villefranche-sur-Saône](https://www.kyriad.com/en/hotels/kyriad-villefranche-sur-saone).
Junction8: Mâcon
1. The Best Western Plus Hotel d'Europe et d'Angleterre is located at Quai Jean Jaurès, Mâcon (71000). You can contact them at +33 3 85 21 90 and find more information on their website [Best Western Mâcon](https://www.bestwestern.fr/en/hotel-Macon-Best-Western-Hotel-d-Europe-et-d-Angleterre-93862).
2. For a pleasant stay in Mâcon, consider the Hôtel Mercure Mâcon Bord de Saône located on Rue Pierre de Coubertin (71000). You can reach them at +33-3-85-39-09 and learn more about this hotel on their website [Mercure Mâcon](https://all.accor.com/hotel/0427/index.fr.shtml).
These hotels are perfect for your Loire Radweg adventure, offering comfortable accommodations at key junctions. For reservations and additional details, please contact the hotels directly.

1. Google Maps:
  - Overview: Google Maps is a widely used and versatile navigation app that offers detailed maps, turn-by-turn navigation, and real-time traffic updates.
   - Features:
    - It provides accurate route planning.
    - You can get real-time traffic conditions.
    - Street view feature allows you to have a visual familiarity with the surroundings.
    - Offline maps are available for areas with weak signal.
    - The app integrates with local businesses and attractions.
2. Komoot:
  - Overview: Komoot is a specialized app designed specifically for cyclists and outdoor enthusiasts. It offers route planning, navigation, and offline maps tailored for biking adventures.
   - Features:
    - The app creates customized cycling routes based on your fitness level.
    - Offline maps are available for remote areas where internet connectivity is limited.
    - You can explore various points of interest along your route.
    - Elevation profiles provide valuable information for informed planning.
    - Turn-by-turn voice navigation ensures you never lose your way.
3. Strava:
  - Overview: Strava is a popular app among cyclists and runners. It focuses on tracking activities, sharing routes, and connecting with a community of like-minded individuals.
   - Features:
    - Track and analyze your activities such as cycling or running.
    - Plan and share routes with other users.
    - Engage in friendly competition through segments feature.

- Connect the app with various devices to enhance your experience

.- Challenges and achievements keep you motivated.

4. Maps.me:

Overview: Maps.me is an offline mapping app that allows users to download detailed maps for offline use. It comes in handy in areas where internet connectivity is limited or unavailable

.- Features:

.- Download entire country's offline maps

.- Detailed points of interest are provided.

.- Get walking, cycling, and driving directions.

.- Bookmark your favorite places and plan routes.

- The maps are up-to-date with community contributions.

5. Ride with GPS:

- Overview: Ride with GPS is a comprehensive app specifically designed for cyclists. It offers route planning, navigation, and tracking features for both road and off-road biking.

- Features:

- Create customizable routes based on your preferences.

- Enjoy turn-by-turn voice navigation to guide you along the way.

- Offline maps are available for remote areas where internet connectivity is limited

.- Track your rides and analyze your performance

.- Explore community-generated routes for new adventures.

Choose the mobile navigation app that suits your preferences and needs to have a seamless and enjoyable experience along the Loire Radweg. Always make sure to update your maps before embarking on your journey.

Local Tourist Information Centers along the Loire Radweg can provide you with valuable information and assistance during your visit. Let's take a closer look at some of these centers:

1. Orléans Tourist Information Center: Located at 2 Place de l'Étape, 45000 Orléans, France, this center is a great resource for all your tourism needs in Orléans. You can reach them at +33 2 38 24 05 05 or visit their website [Orléans Tourist Office](https://www.tourisme-orleans.com/en/) for more information.

2. Tours Tourist Office: Situated at 78-82 Rue Bernard Palissy, 37000 Tours, France, this office is dedicated to providing visitors with comprehensive information about the city of Tours. Feel free to contact them at +33 2 47 70 37 37 or check out their website [Tours Val de Loire Tourist Office](https://www.tours-tourism.co.uk/) for further details.

3. Saumur Tourist Office: Located at 8 Bis Quai Carnot, 49400 Saumur, France, this tourist office offers valuable insights into the enchanting town of Saumur. For any inquiries or assistance, you can reach them at +33 2 41 40 20 or explore their website [Saumur Val de Loire Tourist Office](https://www.ot-saumur.fr/).

4. Angers Tourist Information Center: Positioned at Place du Président Kennedy, Angers, France (49100), this center is dedicated to helping tourists discover the beauty of Angers and its surroundings. To get in touch with them directly, dial +33 (0)241235000 or visit their website [Angers Loire Tourisme](https://www.angersloiretourisme.com/) for more information.

5. Nantes Tourist Office: Located at 9 Rue des États, 44000 Nantes, France, this office is your go-to place for all things related to tourism in Nantes. You can contact them at +33 2 72 640 479 or visit their website [Nantes Tourisme](https://www.nantes-tourisme.com/en) to explore the vibrant city of Nantes.

6. Blois Tourist Office: Situated at 23 Place du Château, Blois, France (41000), this tourist office is dedicated to providing visitors

with valuable information about the charming city of Blois. To get in touch with them, dial +33 2 54 90 41 or visit their website [Blois Chambord - Val de Loire Tourisme](https://www.bloischambord.co.uk/).

7. Tours Val de Loire Airport Tourist Information: If you're arriving at Tours Val de Loire Airport and need assistance or information regarding your visit, you can visit their tourist information center located at 40 Rue de l'Aéroport, Tours, France (37100). For any inquiries or help, feel free to call them at +33 (0)247493737 or check out their website [Tours Val de Loire Airport](https://www.tours.aeroport.fr/).

8. Nevers Tourist Office: Positioned at Rue Sabatier, Nevers, France (58000), this tourist office is a valuable resource for exploring Nevers and its attractions. To contact them directly for any assistance or information needed during your visit, dial +33 (0)386684600 or explore their website [Nevers Magny-Cours Tourisme](https://www.nevers-tourisme.com/).

9. Château de Chambord Visitor Center: If you're planning to visit the magnificent Château de Chambord, make sure to stop by their visitor center located at 41250 Chambord, France. For any inquiries or information about visiting the château, you can contact them at +33 2 54 50 40 or visit their website [Château de Chambord](https://www.chambord.org/).

10. Le Puy-en-Velay Tourist Office: Situated at Place du Clauzel, Le Puy-en-Velay, France (43000), this tourist office is dedicated to providing visitors with all the necessary information and assistance for exploring Le Puy-en-Velay. You can reach them at +33 (0)471093841 or visit their website [Le Puy-en-Velay Tourist Office](https://www.lepuyenvelay-tourisme.fr/en/) for more details.

www.ingramcontent.com/pod-product-compliance
Lightning Source LLC
LaVergne TN
LVHW021157200726
843510LV00001B/417